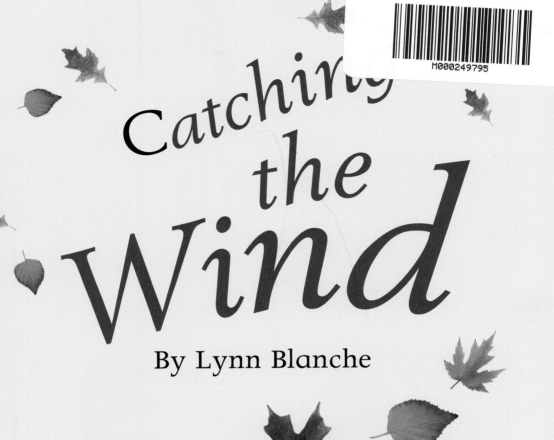

Catching the Wind

By Lynn Blanche

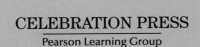

CELEBRATION PRESS
Pearson Learning Group

Contents

What Is Wind?

You can't see it, but you know it's there.
It can rattle the windows on a stormy night.
It can rustle the leaves on trees. It can push you
along the street. What is it? It's the wind.

Wind is moving air. You can't see wind, but you can see the things it does. Because of the wind, seeds scatter. Clothes blow in the breeze. Flags flutter. Pinwheels turn.

Wind creates a **force**. A force is a push or pull that moves things. The force of the wind pushes things, making them move. Wind is what helps lift a kite into the air.

Wind helps a kite rise into the air. The pull of the string keeps the wind from blowing the kite away.

Wind can create different amounts of force. A soft breeze creates a small force. It can blow the seeds off a dandelion. A strong wind creates a large force. It can blow huge tree branches back and forth.

The **Beaufort Scale** measures the strength of the wind. Still air measures 0. Very strong wind measures 12. The scale also shows what can happen when winds of different strengths blow.

The Beaufort Scale

As the numbers get larger, the wind gets stronger.

0 Smoke rises straight up.

1 Smoke drifts.

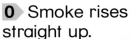

2 Leaves sway.

3 Flags flutter.

4 Paper flies.

5 Medium waves form.

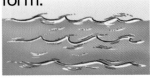

6 Umbrellas turn inside out.

7 Walking is hard.

8–9 Roof shingles blow off.

10–11 Trees are uprooted.

12 Buildings are destroyed.

Wind Helps Sailboats Move

Wind helps sailboats move through water. Sometimes the wind pushes on the sail. Other times it blows across the sail. A sailor can change the position of the sail to catch the wind and make the boat move.

Long ago, sailing ships carried people and items
to many countries. Ships often had many sails
to catch the wind. There was a problem with
sailing ships, however. If the wind didn't blow,
the ships could not move.

In the 1800s ships like this
carried tea and other items
to many areas of the world.

Today many kinds of sailboats don't have to count on wind power alone. They also have engines. If the wind dies, power from the engine can move the boat along.

Wind Helps People Work

Long ago people used big stones to grind grain into flour. Turning the heavy stones was hard work. Later people figured out how to use the wind to do the work for them. They built windmills.

It often took two people to grind grain into flour.

Windmills were invented hundreds of years ago.

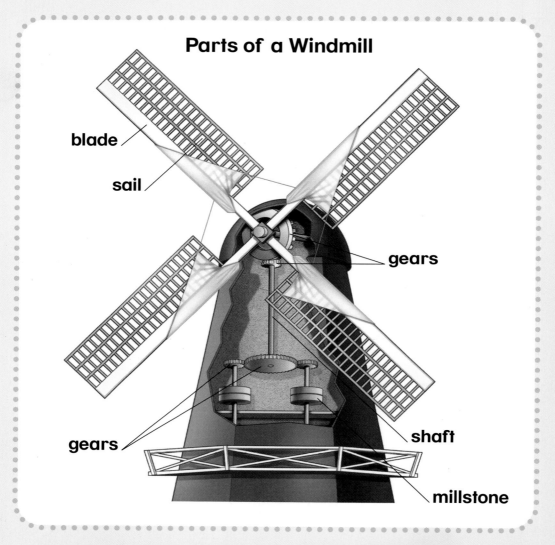

Parts of a Windmill

blade

sail

gears

gears

shaft

millstone

How did a windmill work? The wind blew on the sails. That made the blades turn. The blades were connected to a shaft and gears. When they turned, so did the **millstones**. They ground the grain.

Today windmills still help people in some places grind grain. People also use **wind turbines**. Wind turbines use wind power to make **electricity**. The electricity can be used to run many different machines.

Wind blows the blades of a wind turbine and makes them turn.

Wind Farms

Places where many wind turbines work together are called **wind farms**. Wind farms are located in very windy places. Many are on open plains.

Too Much Wind

Sometimes wind power can be harmful. Strong winds can break tree branches, knock down fences, and cause huge waves.

The winds in **tornadoes** and in storms like **hurricanes** are dangerous. They can uproot trees, send cars flying, and even flatten houses.

A hurricane in Puerto Rico destroyed this building.

Still, wind isn't always dangerous. People use wind to fly kites, hang glide, sail, and windsurf. Wind power helps people have fun!

Glossary

Beaufort Scale   a tool used to measure wind power

electricity   a kind of energy that makes machines and lights work

force   a push or pull that moves things

hurricanes   powerful storms that form over warm water

millstones   big stones used to grind grain into flour

tornadoes   severe windstorms shaped like twisting, spinning funnels; form mostly over land

wind farms   places where a number of wind turbines are grouped together

wind turbines   tall towers with large, spinning blades that are used to make electricity